INSPIRATION:
A Woman's Spiritual Triumph

Other Works by Aurora Wilson Available for Purchase

Visit: www.amazon.com/author/AuroraWilson

* The Missing Piece in Business
* Step Into Your Vision 2.0 featuring Les Brown, John Assaraf, and other Inspirational Business Leaders
* Family Ties
* How to Self-Motivate – Inspirational Guide for Growth
* Tips to Began a Life Coach Career
* The Missing Piece in Forgiveness

Upcoming Books

* The Awakening Moment
* Healing Prayers: Believe and Achieve
* Daily Devotions
* Smart, Sexy, and Saved

INSPIRATION:
A Woman's Spiritual Triumph

A book of quotes, prayers, thoughts, and prose

Aurora Wilson
By Aurora Wilson Global and Ministries

DEDICATION

This book is dedicated to the memory of my late son, Dante Markeith Steele. You left this earth much too soon. Forever my heart and spirit will remember you, until we meet again. I will make you proud.

-Love Mom

This book is dedicated to my late Grand-mother, Erma Nash Bryant who lost the battle with breast cancer May 2011. Your life and legacy that followed were not in vain. For your love and constant support I am forever grateful.

-Love Aurora

CONTENTS

ACKNOWLEDGEMENTS

This book, and all my work, could not be possible without the encouragement, guidance, compassion and loving support of my family and friends who inspired me to become the best me for me and fulfill my purpose in life.

To my sons, Meurisse Wilson and Davon Steele, I love you both and thank you.

To my mom, Michele Williams, thanks for your support and love.

Finally, but certainly not least, I would like to thank God, my heavenly father above for making this book possible. I am grateful that readers will have a tool they can pick up each day as a resource.

I would like to thank all those that have assisted me during the many seasons of my life.

ABOUT INSPIRATION THE BOOK

Inspiration: A Woman's Spiritual Triumph is a book of prayer, thoughts, prose and quotes. This book is for all human beings who are striving for strength, restoration and healing during any phase in their life. I pray this book be a source of strength and encouragement for your life.

I am thankful that I am able to help so many with the words within these pages.

I am forever grateful that my journey can help you along on your journey.

ABOUT THE AUTHOR

Author Aurora Wilson, known as Pastor Light, is a certified professional life coach, motivational speaker, healthcare advocate, and ordained minister. Her goal is that through her writing, teaching, and coaching that she will inspire many through direction and testimony to live their best life; which is ultimately an awakened experience, which they were born to live.

The author resides in Florida where she enjoys spending time with her family, grandchildren, and assisting others in reaching their awakening moment and fulfilling their life purpose.

She is the co-founder/partner of iCoach & Co, co-founder of Christian Women Speakers Association, State Project Leader for the National Patient Advocate Foundation, Owner of Aurora Health Advocates and Aurora Wilson Ministries and Dean of Students for I Am A Ruby Ministries School.

She is the mother of 2 sons and 4 grandchildren. She tragically lost her youngest son January 2013 due to violence.

WALKING THE WALK

Your journey will lead you to new roads paths
Hills and valleys that you never imagined you'd walk
The goal is not to avoid these walks
But to endure, grow and learn from them
This is the only way you will free yourself
From walking the same road again

God I ask you on this day
That no matter what is occurring in my life
That I move
That I smile
That I continue to know
That you are here by my side
I ask you God
On this trying day
That no matter what may occur
That I will be brave and hold on to your word
I thank you today for allowing me to walk
To move forward
To embrace courage
I thank you for these limbs

I love being a woman
I just love everything about being a woman
I love walking the walk of a woman
Gliding the glide of a woman
Bearing the strength of a woman
Being wise, oh so wise
I just love this woman looking back in the mirror
For she is strong
Oh yes, she is strong

I am embracing the fact that every day may not be a yes
But I am alive
Therefore the word no does not scare me
I embrace it
I have learned to love it
Because every no has gotten me closer to a lifetime of
YES!

I am still moving
I have had heartbreaks
I have had pain
But I am still moving
I have been disappointed
Used and abused
But I continue to walk
My legs are sometimes heavy
As is my burdens
But I move
And God lightens my load
I am still moving
I am still moving
Walking the walk
I am walking the walk

Just when I thought I would not make it
My breakthrough knocked on my front door

Psalms 23
Has gotten me through a few dark hours
Not a shot of Vodka
Or a Cigar
Could replace the flavor of an on time God

MY SPIRITUAL JOURNEY

My spiritual journey has led me to the unknown

The unseen

The edge of hope

Is where I have landed

And arrived into the woman I was meant to be all along

I am and have become the being

I have been praying for

I am

And I am becoming all things through God's grace

My prayer for you today is that you will allow your journey
to become

Walk into it

Take the first step towards a future promised to you

Allow your journey to begin

Commence on the notion of faith

Pause on the notion of fear

Embrace all that is unknown

Face it bravely

And walk

Arrive in your journey

And may you end up as yourself

Home
Home is where I have always belonged
Home
Is where I am loved
Home
Is where I heal
Home
Is where my family resides
Home
Is where I belong
Home
I am headed home

It has been since forever that I allowed a circumstance to control the destiny that is waiting for me

And you know what

It will be forever and a day until I ever allow

A thing

A person

An action

A circumstance

To stop the power that I hold

The power that I own

It has been forever

And a day

That I gave something else my power

The transference of power occurs when you take back all the
enemy took… it is time to regain what is rightfully yours

You deserve to make mistakes
This simply means that you have tried
You are allowed to cry
This simply means that you have felt
You are allowed to tune out
This means that you have tuned into self
You, yes you
You are allowed
To become all that you have dreamed
You deserve
A life that is worth living
You deserve this journey
For this journey is your very own
Enjoy it

I am grateful for all the experience that have taught me

Showed me

Stretched me

Tested me

But it has made me

Me

And for this I am forever grateful

If my ancestors could see me now…

They would smile

They would be proud

The walls of my heritage would make a beat from a powerful drum

And smile at where the road has led me

If my ancestors could see me now

They would smile

Yes, they would smile

I realize that I have a gift
A gift
A specific appointment that only I can fulfill
According to James 1:17-18
Every good and perfect gift is from above
I look up and I am lifted
I reach high and I am elevated

PRAYERS

Dear God,

I say a prayer for healing the past

Today I pray for those that are in pain from their past
I ask you in your holy name that you may release them and free them of their past
Give their future a purpose that only they can fulfill.
Feel hope in the hearts of the hurting Lord so that their journey may continue

Morning Prayer

It is a new day

I ask you God that I do not carry the cares of yesterday into today

Use me today in a powerful mighty way

So that someone today will be touched by my presence

It is a new day

I will control all that I can

And what I cannot control I will leave to you God

I realize that I cannot handle everything on my own

I also recognize that I am not supposed to

I love and thank you for today

Midday Prayer

Father the day seems to slip away from me

There are times I do not know how I am going to accomplish
all I set out to do

But I trust in you and know that you have given me the right
time

The right hours and the right season to do all that you have
called me to do

I thank you for strength in this season and for the days to
come

A Prayer

Loneliness on the journey

There are times when I feel alone

No family, friends or even success can quench my need to feel wanted and desired

Sometimes I hurt by the people that have left me and abandoned me

I thank you for the people you have removed from my life

I trust that you know what is best for me

I thank you for the doors you have closed

And the new doors that you are opening

Based on your word

And according to **Jeremiah 29:11**, I know that you have a future hope for me

There are days that are longer than others

But I know that because you love me I am never alone

And with this I am able to continue my journey.

A Prayer for God's Love

Love

You are the greatest journey

The most acquired knowledge

On this walk in my life

I have experienced so many levels of you

Love

You are the one constant truth that remains

Love

You are what this world needs more of

Love

Love

Love

You are what I feel

I Say A Prayer for Your Life's Challenges

God I thank you

For the human being reading this prayer

They need to know that you are present in the midst of their storm

They need to know that their season of challenge, turmoil and storms are over

They need to understand that you are building their character

And that character is needed for the places they have yet seen

I am grateful that in this season that Gods people will trust you God and not their circumstances

I am thankful that their tears will dry

That their hurt will heal

And that this challenge will be their greatest reward in the future

A Prayer for Betrayal

It pains the heart and soul when family, close friends and
those we trust betray us

They turn against the love we trusted them with

Our hearts become sullen

Our spirits become damaged

But greater we are in you Christ

That you have come to heal us

You have come to rescue us from pain

God send restoration to families that are broken

Send healing to hearts that are hurting

Send a word of kindness to a closed ear

God we ask you for peace right now and always

THE AWAKENING MOMENT

Today
I experienced an awakening
The skies opened
The moon shun
Today
Oh yes today
I experienced an awakening like no other
My soul jumped leaps and bounds
My spirit awakened to a new me
Today
Oh yes today
Was not like any other day
Something within me changed

It is time

It is my season

My season to step into the woman I was meant to become

It is my season

It is my time

History will become as I am determined to make it

I am alive with truth

I am awakened with a new purpose

This is my journey

This is my time

This is my awakening moment

Remember, what consumes you controls you
You can say that you are over something
But the more you relive it
Bitterness will settle in
The more you speak about it
Is the more you give the negative energy in your life power
Remember
What consumes you controls you
And what controls you grows within you
Choose wisely

Be kind to yourself
After all there is only one
You

What I know for sure is this
God makes no mistakes
When one door closes, it is because God is waiting to open a
million new doors

I surrender to this process

This process called life

Beginning your day with prayer and reflection will assist you from worrying about a day that you cannot control. Remember God is in control. Allow the spirit to lead and guide you

They say

Sometimes

Or often times

Words are misused

Two of them being

Love and Friend

You cannot tell someone's story without knowing the entire book

Reading all the pages

Introduction, outline

And only then can you turn the page to their life

But we can never finish someone's story when we are completing our own

Integrity

It's more than a word

It is greater than a shadow to hide after

Integrity

It is greater than your looks, finances and success

If you lack integrity

You lack character

And without character you will be destroyed

Be brave
Because in the end
It will all work in your favor

To get to where you need to be
You'll have to do what you have to do
Even when you do not want to

Think of today as the best day of your life
And live accordingly

For certain
In this life
The only thing that is consistent is
God

Devil you should be afraid
I am a child of the most high God
And I am walking in my greatness

A NEW SEASON, A NEW DAY

Prose, thoughts, quotes & prayers about a new season coming

A person who lacks a grateful spirit is like a snake that poisons the spirit
And bites the hands that have fed them with love

So as you think
So it shall be

Some of Gods greatest gifts are unanswered prayers

The thing I love most about God is that when he doesn't answer a prayer
He always shows you why eventually

The difference between an opportunist and a person seeking a new opportunity is

One plants, while the other, plots

Prayer changes things even if we do not see it

I have never been interested in a career

My goal has always been to set my path on a purpose filled fire

Every day I find another reason to trust God

Never return to your past

Not even for a visit

There is a reason God removed this event from your life the first time around

I will always stay true to what I believe
Even if it means standing alone

God made us all so rich that he gave us the sea
The sea has no worries
The sea has no ending
The sea belongs to us all

No matter how many times you fall
Stand up and keep walking towards the road to your dreams

God is able
Even when you are not
He is able

Dear Misery,

Thanks for the invitation to join you.
But I respectfully decline the offer.

Signed,
A Winner and Champion

You will never find what you are looking for
If you are looking for it in others

A Prayer For a Parent Who Has Loss a Child

A fish cannot function outside of water

Its natural habitat

The ocean is like the womb of a mother

And the loss of a child

Can be compared to the same

Living after the loss of a child is like roaming this earth without oxygen

You do

But it is trying and downright difficult

But you go on

You keep living, as with the spirit of your children

My child will always be in the memory of my heart

Everyone has bad days
That is why God makes new days

When you are headed in the right direction God will always
give you confirmation

Change is coming
Stay faithful because God sees you right where you are
You are not abandoned or alone

One thing I have learned about life
Is that it goes on
You have no choice but to continue moving forward

FREESTYLE

This portion of the book is for the freedom in God, freedom in purpose, and having freedom in the awakened self.

When God is testing you in a big way
It is because he is ready to use you in a big way

You must get up each day
And awake your spirit

Which is more important?
Your purpose or your problem
Whichever you give energy to will grow

God can do miracles in your life
Keep your trust in him

Things will get pretty ugly
In fact, pretty difficult
Right before beautiful is birthed
Just wait
Things will revolve in a beautiful mess

You are going to make it because God said you are

Yesterday is gone
All the mistakes, problems, frustrations associated with it are gone
All you have is today
This moment
Make the most of it by leaving yesterday in the past

No matter what you are facing
God will always give you a new sunrise and sunset
Always look for the good in things
It is there you will find peace

When God decides that you are number one
There is no force that can change this certainty

God is a restorer
So thank him for what you loss
A double portion of what you loss is coming back your way
Be prepared to receive your double portion

You were made the way you are

Not by accident

Do not allow this world to tell you that God made a mistake
in you

Nope… you are perfect just the way you are

Everything that is given to you

Should be returned to the universe

Sow

Reap

And so it flows

Instead of thinking what can I get out of this?

Think what can I give out of this situation

There is not waste
It all happened for a reason
Look what you have come through
The mirror should read victor
Not victim

It will continue to be hard to see the good in others
If you do not first learn to see it in yourself
We all have work to do

Walk away swiftly
From anything which no longer serves a purpose in your life

The number one way not to block your blessings
Is to learn how to celebrate others blessings

I have learned to never worry
Because God is an on time God

I'd rather walk into greatness
Than settle for good
Life is all about choices
Make the decision to be great

A Prayer For Today

Today
Is going to be a great day
Because it is today
Receive it
Claim it
You were born to win
You are here to fulfill a great purpose on earth
You were born to stand out

A Prayer For Tragedy

In life
No matter what happened
The only time tragedy occurs is if you give up
Keep pushing
God we ask that you may give us the strength
To persevere
That through you we may understand
That we are able
We are able because you are able
We are possible because you are the God of possibilities
Father I call on you today
For unspeakable strength
I speak life into this matter

Thank you God for the breakthrough that is coming

Hopelessness says give up

Doubt questions the possibility

But faith knows that with vision, believing and action it will happen

Today I believe that favor and grace is following me

Who believes with me?

Grace is flowing within me

Grace is showing outside of me

And because of grace I can make it another day

And for this I am grateful

A Faithful Challenge For The Day

Today only words of faith will come from my mouth
Who is up for the challenge with me?
I will not speak in doubt
Fear will have no room here
Today
Only faith will live within me

No matter that the journey looks like
Or where the road has led
I have learned to trust the process
And that has made all the difference

Everyone is looking for the next big thing
But so many do not realize that the next big thing is already
here
It's within

In this life
One of the biggest battles you will fight will be within
You might as well get to work

The more you fall in love with yourself
Is the more the world will embrace what you see
It is time to change your inward mirror image

God is so generous that he gave us all the same twenty-four
hours in a day
So why is it that some accomplish great task
Some mediocre
And others do not have a task
Choices
Priorities

The very day I changed my mind
Was the very day I changed my life
That is truly all it took

I learned to believe to the point of optimistic insanity
You should believe to the point that people will wonder in
awe
Is it possible to have that much faith?
Why, yes it is!

Never trust what it looks like
Rarely trust what the circumstance says
Trust what God says

Fear and faith has the same goal in mind
They both want you to believe in them
Which will you believe?

You can analyze the door your entire life
Wait for its handle to cool in temperature
Or you can boldly walk through the door in faith

Never let your enemy know that you are aware that they are
your enemy
Instead break bread with them
Pray for them
And before long they will call you friend
And you have won the silent war so many lose

I have learned to embrace myself freely and fully
It was not until I learned that everything was right with me
That life became one big yes
Say yes to yourself and life will say yes back

God can deliver us from any situation
The miracle is not in the deliverance
But in trusting he will deliver you

You are greater than what has happened to you
You are exactly who God declared you to become

With every dream you are going to have to fight to see it
come to pass
I wish I could tell you a lie
Like it is all a walk in a spring-seasoned park
It's sometimes a cold winter
But your dream is greater than any storm

Do not go around allowing what hurt you to stop you
What hurt you taught you what did not work in your life
Now move on to the things that are working
Do not stay stuck

Some will wonder why they cannot get ahead
It is because the luggage they are carrying from the past is
too heavy to carry
You're going to have to let some things go in order to walk
into your promise

A Final Prayer

God I thank you for every person that has read this book

That their lives may be transformed daily

That a new person

With a new mind will arrive

I pray that through these pages a new person have awakened

I love and thank you father for every individual that was lost
but now has guidance

That was hurting but now has begun to heal

Whose heart was heavy but is now light

God give people a vision for their lives

A purpose that will set them on fire for life

Keep them excited on their journey

Bless their journey

NOTES

This book is a Collection of Thoughts, LLC creation ghostwritten by Justinah McFadden

Made in the USA
Middletown, DE
27 December 2017